WINDOWS ON OUR WORLD

HOUGHTON MIFFLIN SOCIAL STUDIES

Me
At Home, At School
In Our Community
Ourselves and Others
Our Home, the Earth
America: Past and Present
Around Our World

GENERAL EDITOR
Lee F. Anderson

Frank L. Ryan
Lynne S. Schwab

Houghton Mifflin Company   Boston

Atlanta   Dallas   Geneva, Illinois   Hopewell, New Jersey   Palo Alto   Toronto

At Home, At School

ABOUT THE AUTHORS

Frank L. Ryan is Professor of Education at the University of California at Riverside. He has served as consultant for school districts in California, South Dakota, Nebraska, and Minnesota. A former elementary-level demonstration teacher, Frank Ryan has contributed many articles to professional journals. He is author of *Exemplars for the New Social Studies, The Social Studies Source Book,* and co-author of *Instructional Implications of Inquiry.*

Lynne S. Schwab is Associate Professor of Education at the University of North Florida. She has taught in the elementary schools of California, and has had wide experience as a consultant for federally funded early childhood, social studies, and teacher-training projects, including the training of teachers at Quinalt and Navajo schools.

Cover and Title Page Photo: Jim Cartier; Photo Researchers, Inc.
                Cover Map: Susan Lexa

ISBN: 0-395-27462-1

GENERAL EDITOR

Lee F. Anderson is Professor of Education and Political Science at Northwestern University and Chairman of the American Political Science Association, Committee on Pre-Collegiate Education. His numerous published articles and papers include the frequently reprinted "Global Education: Long Range Goals and Objectives." He is a member of the Social Science Education Consortium and the National Council for the Social Studies.

GENERAL CONSULTANTS

Charlotte C. Anderson is on the staff of the American Bar Association's Special Committee on Youth Education for Citizenship. In this position she directs regional and national conferences and serves as a consultant for civic education programs. She formerly directed the teacher education program at Northwestern University and is the author of many articles on social education.

Barbara J. Winston is Associate Professor and Chairperson, Department of Geography and Environmental Studies at Northeastern Illinois University. She is also engaged in the university's teacher education program. Previously she taught in the Palatine and Park Ridge, Illinois, public school systems.

READING CONSULTANT

Roger E. Johnson is Professor of Education and Chairman of the Social Science/Letters Department at the University of South Florida. He is an elementary social studies consultant for Florida public schools and a reading adviser to a number of local school systems.

EDITORIAL ADVISER

Howard D. Mehlinger is Professor of History and Education at Indiana University and serves as Editorial Adviser for Houghton Mifflin Social Studies programs.

CONTENTS

1
You and Me

How do we look?

Do I look like you?

How are we different from one another?

Do I look different from you?

We look alike.
We look different.

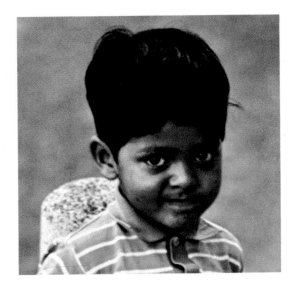

15

How do we feel?

When are we happy?

1

2

3

4

When are we sad?

What makes us afraid?

Being afraid is no fun.
What can we do?

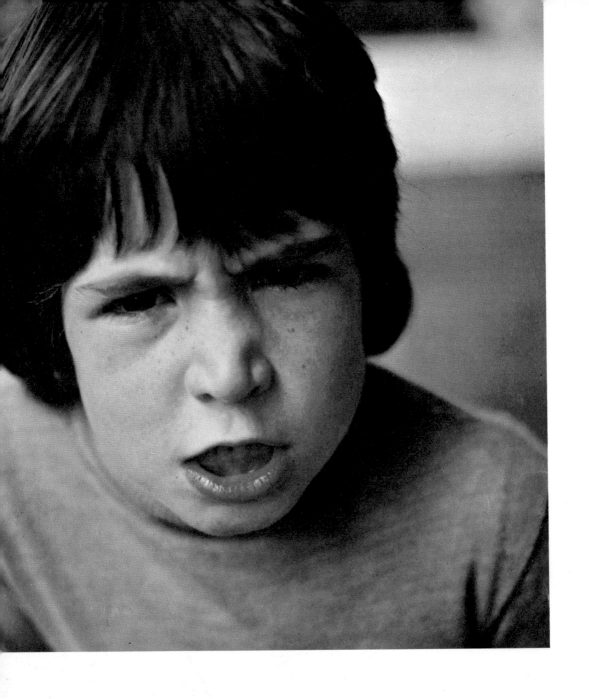

When do we feel this way?

What can we do to keep from being angry?

I like myself.

You like yourself.

We are alike.

We are different.

1

4

2

3

5

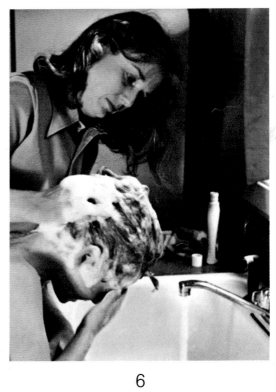

6

What if . . .

Why is it good to be alike?

What if . . .

Why is it good to be different?

How are we alike?

How are we different?

2
Our Needs

What are living things?

You and I are living things.

Which of these are living things?
Which is most like you and me?

Which are living things?

Which of them grew?

Which need food and water?

Which need air?

Which need rest?

43

What keeps us safe and warm?

What keeps them safe and warm?

How are people like other living things?

47

3
People

People talk.

Tell this story.

What comes next?

Who can tell a story?

What are these people telling us?

Tony lives on Main Street.
How will he know which bus to take?

What do these tell us?

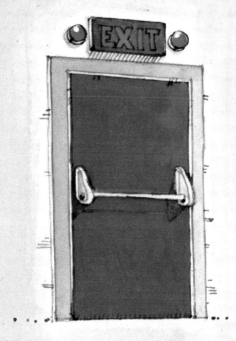

My friend cannot see.

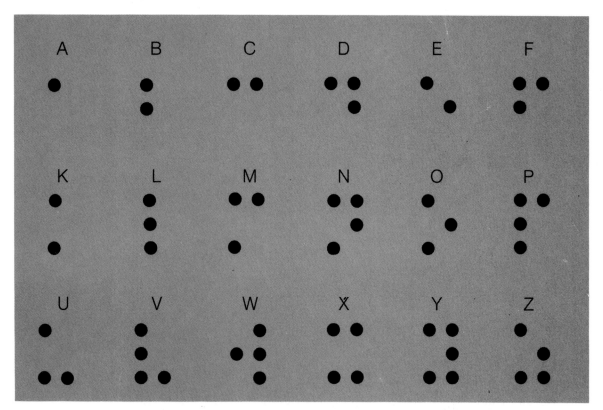

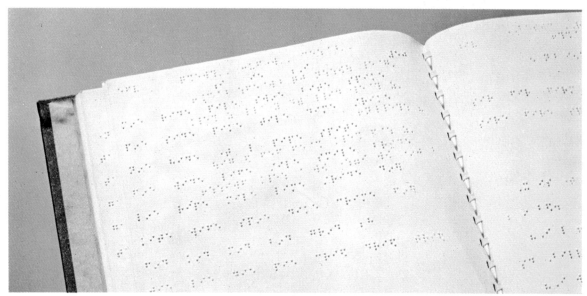

How can she read stories?

Your friends cannot hear.

How can you tell them a story?

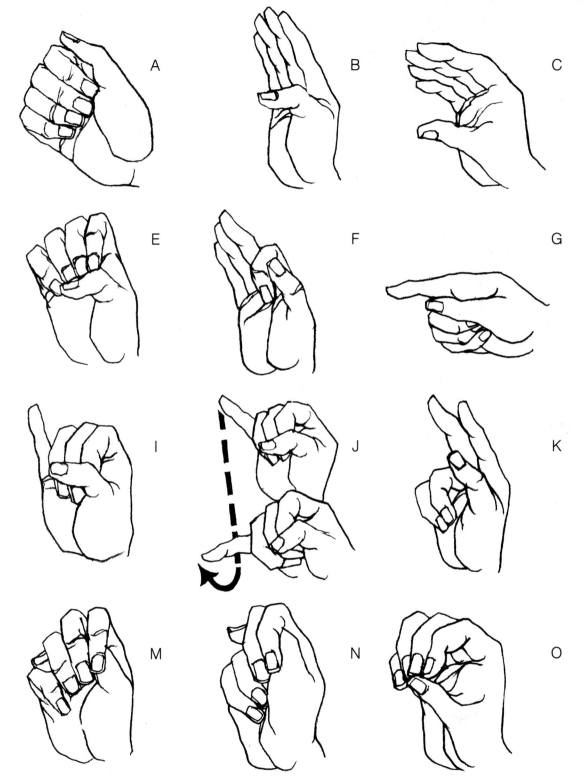

A   B   C

E   F   G

I   J   K

M   N   O

People make tools.

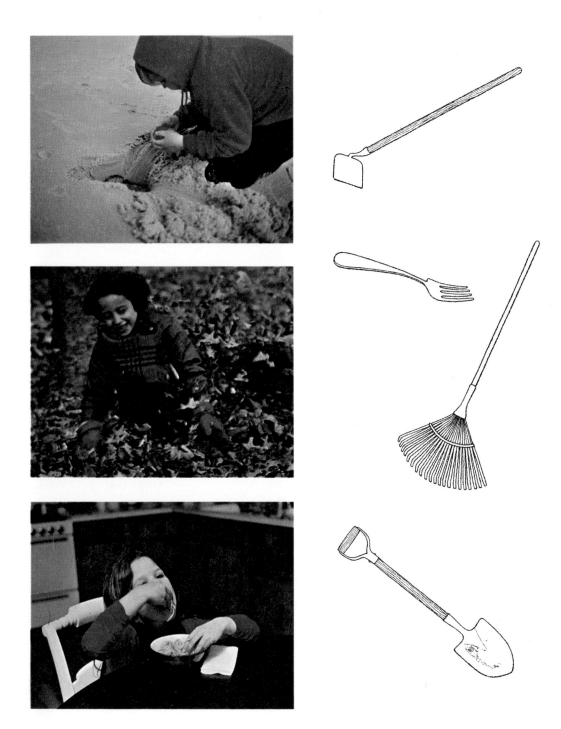

What tool would you use?

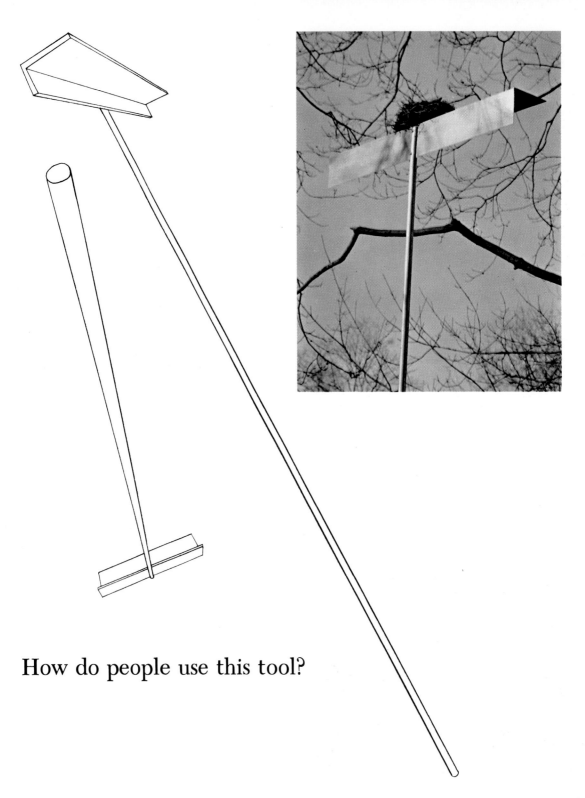

How do people use this tool?

63

Which are using tools?

Can you make a tool?

People think and choose.

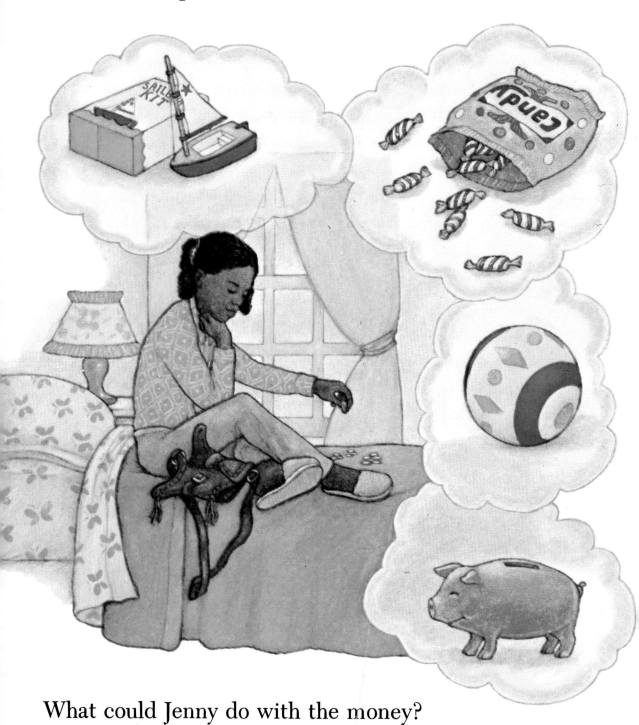

What could Jenny do with the money?

What did she do with it?

Billy does not like to put on boots.

If he puts on boots . . .

If he does not put on boots . . .

What will Billy do?

70

Why did Sara say, "No"?

What are these people doing?

How are people different from other living things?

4
Families

We live in families.

Families are alike.
Families are different.

77

How does your family help you?

Families work together.

Who is helping?

Who is not helping?

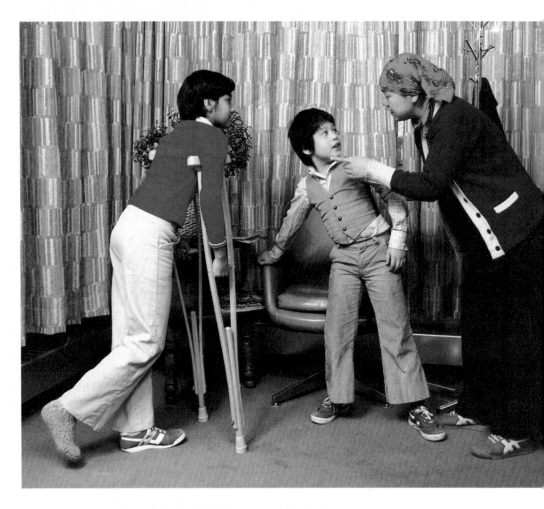

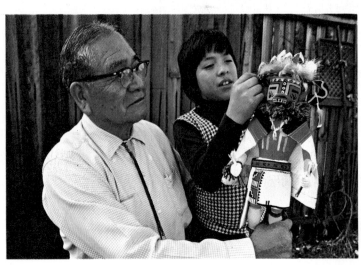

Who is learning?
Who is teaching?

84

What are these families doing?
What days are special to them?

Families sometimes fight.

Who will play with the blocks?

Who will wash the dishes?

What will they do?

What is happening?
What would you do?

Families need other people.

What does this family want to buy?

What people do they need?

Jane wants a bike.

Why can't Jane have a bike?

How is this family like yours?

How is it different?

5
Schools

We go to school.

What do we learn?

What work does she do?

Where did she learn to do it?

How are these schools like yours?

How are they different?

People in schools work together.

How do these people help one another?
How do they help you?

Schools need money.

What do schools buy?

What is she doing?
Why must she choose?

The children are going to school.

Who pays for the school?

111

Schools have rules.

What rules are these children following?

Why do schools have rules?

What rule would you make?

What makes a rule a good rule?

115

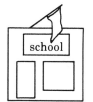

What is a school?

6
Using Space

How is space used?

What is in the space above the house?

What is in the space under the tree?

Where is the dog?

What is in the space by the window?

What is in the space near the table?

Where is the baby?

How are these people using space?

How are these living things using space?

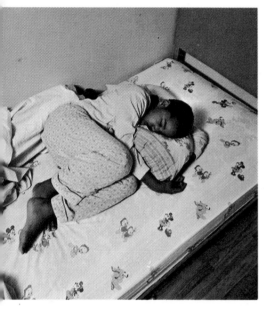

Which is using more space?

When do living things use more space?

Are these the same classroom?

How do you know?

What is different?

What happens in the classroom?

How would you use the classroom space?

Why?

How would you use this space?

Plan 1

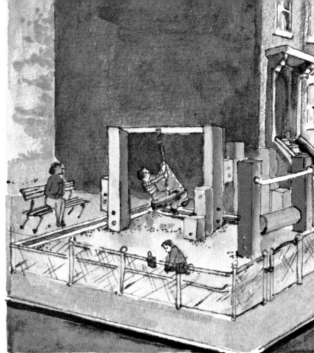

Plan 2

Plan 3

Plan 4

What do models show us?

Find the models.

What kind of room is this?

How do you know?

What is the girl doing?

What does the model show us?

Can you make a model of your classroom?

What do maps show us?

This is the model the girl made.

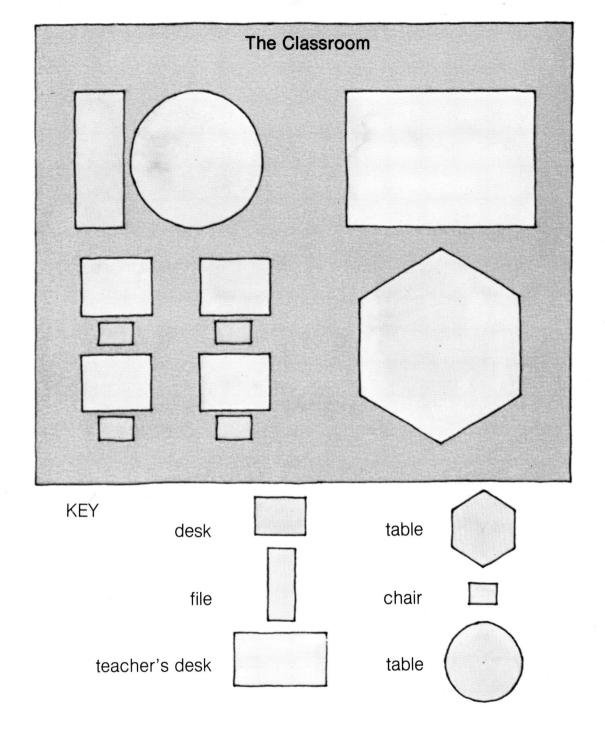

The Classroom

KEY

desk

file

teacher's desk

table

chair

table

This is a map of her classroom.
How would you change the map?

136

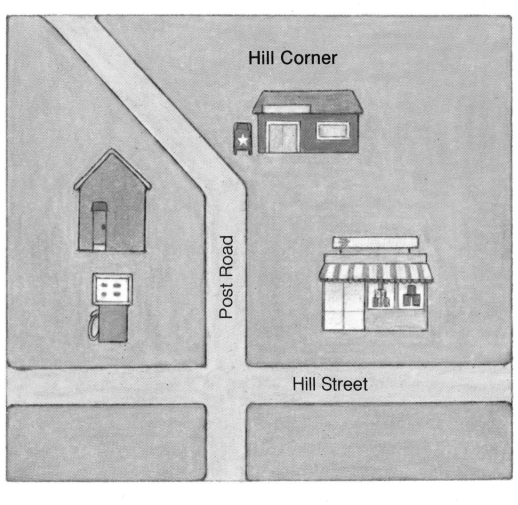

Hill Corner

Post Road

Hill Street

KEY

house  post office

gas food store

How are they alike?

How are they different?

This is a picture of Lake Park.

KEY

bench   ball field

lake   sandbox

tree   swings

What does the map show you?

How is it like the picture?

How is it different?

Word List

afraid		family	
alike		happy	
angry		help	
choose		holiday	
different		learn	

living things

sad

map

school

model

space

money

think

rule

tool

CREDITS

The authors and publisher wish to express their appreciation to persons and organizations listed below for their courtesy in preparing illustrations and in making photographs available for reproduction. The following abbreviations have been used for a few sources from which many photographs were obtained: Stock—Stock, Boston; PR—Photo Researchers; NAS—National Audubon Society; EPA—Editorial Photocolor Archives.

ILLUSTRATIONS

Mark Bellerose: 20
Marie DeJohn: 34–35, 66–67, 94–95, 136–137
Ethel Gold: 60, 61, 87, 91, 92–93, 114–115, 140–141
Ken Longtemps: 59, 62
Susan Mohn: 22–23, 78–79, 129
Diane Paterson: 70–71, 96–97
Karen Pellaton: 50–51, 106–107, 110–111, 138, 139
Channing Thieme: 27, 57(top)
Joel Snyder: 32–33, 54–55, 68–69, 88–89, 108–109, 120–121, 135

ASSIGNMENT PHOTOGRAPHY

Bohdan Hrynewych: 72–73, 90, 103(bottom left), 112(bottom right)
Lou Jones: 112(top), 128
Carol Palmer/Andy Brilliant: 76(top), 84(top), 98, 99
Frank Siteman/John Urban: 24, 26, 56, 57(bottom), 58, 62, 63(all), 65, 86, 102(top), 126(all), 127(all), 130, 132, 133, 134
Daniel D. Sullivan: 25(top), 28, 31(bottom right), 64(bottom), 81(bottom)
Bonnie Unsworth: 8–9, 21(both), 25(bottom), 30(bottom right), 81(top), 82(top), 83(bottom), 112(left), 116, 117(bottom)
Peter Vadnai: 31(top right), 60(bottom), 113

RESEARCH PHOTOGRAPHY

10   Cary Wolinsky, Stock
11   Cary Wolinsky, Stock
12   Peter Vadnai, EPA
13   Owen Franken, Stock
14   L. L. T. Rhodes, Taurus(top left); Owen Franken, Stock(top right); Marjorie Pickens(bottom left); Henry Deters, Monkmeyer(bottom right)
15   Frank Siteman(top left); Michal Heron(top right); Frank Siteman(bottom left)
16   Bill Anderson, Monkmeyer
17   Rudi Robinson(top left); Bonnie Unsworth(top right); B. I. Ullman, Taurus(bottom left); Paul Conklin, Monkmeyer(bottom right)
18   Barry Hennings, PR
19   Owen Franken, Stock(top); Michal Heron, Monkmeyer(bottom)
29   Frank Siteman
30   Bonnie Unsworth(top)
31   Peter Arnold(top left); Mimi Forsyth, Monkmeyer(bottom left)
36–37   Carol Palmer/Andy Brilliant
38   Marjorie Pickens
39   George Sheng(top left); J. Lesser, Bruce Colemen(top right); Molly Heron(bottom)
40   George Sheng(top left); Erika Stone, Peter Arnold(top right); Russ Kine, PR(bottom left); Dr. E. R. Degginger(bottom right)
41   PR(top left); George Sheng(top right); Peter Arnold(bottom left); Owen Franken, Stock(bottom right)
42   Rosemary Scott, Taurus
43   Paula Rhodes/Joe Nucci(top left); Dr. E. R. Degginger(top right); Ken Heyman(bottom)
44   Frank Siteman, Stock(top); Peter Vandermark(bottom left); Moscati/Joan Kramer(bottom right)
45   Stephen Collins, NAS(top); John M. Burnley, Bruce Coleman(bottom left); Rod Borland, Bruce Coleman(bottom right)
46   Dr. E. R. Degginger(top); Hal H. Harrison, Grant Heilman (bottom left); Walter Chandoha(bottom right)
47   Gabor Demjen, Stock(top left); Erik Anderson(top right); Jacques Jongoux(bottom)
48–49   Bonnie Unsworth
52   Michal Heron(top); Yoram Kanaha, Peter Arnold(bottom)
53   Gove, Photo Trends(top); Joel Sternfeld(bottom)
60   Peter Vandermark(top); Marion Bernstein(middle)
61   George Sheng(top); Malcolm McConahy, NAS(middle); Evelyne Appel(bottom)
64   Harry Engels, PR(top left); Ralph A. Reinhold, Animals, Animals(top right)
74–75   Bill Binzen
76   Mimi Forsyth, Monkmeyer(top right); Peter Vandermark, Stock(bottom)
77   David Strickler, Monkmeyer(top left); Margot Granitsas, PR(bottom left); Michal Heron, Monkmeyer(bottom right)
80   David Strickler, Monkmeyer(left); Rogers, Monkmeyer(right)
81   Rich Medved, Taurus(bottom right)
83   Rhoda Sidney, Monkmeyer(top)
84   Bruce Roberts, PR(bottom)
85   Jacques Jongoux(top); Lou Jones(bottom)
100–101   Four by Five
102   Titmus, Taurus(bottom)
103   Marcia Nichols(top); Norman Prince(middle right)
104   Jim Harrison, Stock
105   Rudi Robinson(top right); Jim Holland, Stock(middle left); Shostal(bottom right)
117   Marcia Nichols(top left); Mimi Forsyth, Monkmeyer(top right)
118–119   Norman Prince
122   EPA(top left); Neil Leifer for Sports Illustrated © TIME, Inc.(top right); Donald Dietz, Stock(bottom left); Cary Wolinsky, Stock(bottom right)
123   Breck Kent, Animals Animals(top left); Paula Rhodes/Joe Nucci(top right); Dr. E. R. Degginger(bottom left); C. W. Perkins, Animals Animals(bottom right)
124   H. L. Gunderson, NAS(top right)
125   Walter Chandoha(top left); Marjorie Pickens(top right); Jacques Jangoux(bottom left and right)
131   Marcia Nichols

ABCDEFGHIJ-D-854321O/79

142